The world is my country

A celebration of the people and movements that opposed the First World War in 10 posters and stories

Emily Johns & Gabriel Carlyle

PEACE NEWS PRESS · FEBRUARY 2015

The world is my country by Emily Johns and Gabriel Carlyle
ISBN 978 0 946409 18 1
Pictures: © Emily Johns
Text: © Gabriel Carlyle

Published in 2015 by Peace News Press
5 Caledonian Road
London N1 9DY

Published since 1936, *Peace News* works for a nonviolent world –
where war has been abolished and the roots of war pulled up,
including the silent routine violence of hunger, oppression and
ecological devastation. Drawing on the traditions of pacifism, feminism,
anarchism, socialism, human rights, animal rights and green politics –
without dogma, but in the spirit of openness – *Peace News* seeks to
create positive change based on co-operation and responsibility.
For more information see **www.peacenews.info**

Printed by Fastprint, St Leonards-on-Sea, East Sussex
Design by Erica Smith, wordsmithdesign.co.uk

FOR ESME,
ARKADY AND
SONIA

Contents

10 things you might not know…

According to two recent polls, while most people think they know either 'a lot' (6%) or 'a fair amount' (45%) about the history of the First World War, almost every fact about the conflict is known to only a minority of the public.[1]

So, as the Government and right-wing historians attempt to write their own tendentious narratives onto this largely blank slate, we offer our own list of 10 intriguing things about the war that you might not know…

1 Occupation, massacre and imperial exploitation by European countries and the US were commonplace in the years leading up to the war. *See pp. 16–20.*

2 Across Britain, probably over 100,000 people took part in peace demonstrations on 2 August 1914, two days before Britain declared war on Germany. *See p. 28.*

3 British policy makers had a hidden war aim in 1914, 'made plain in their private deliberations'[2] but concealed from the public. *See p. 23.*

4 By 1917 an estimated one-third of military-age Quakers in Britain had enlisted. *See p. 30.*

5 Gandhi actively supported the war, and tried to recruit 12,000 Indians to serve as soldiers. *See p. 84.*

6 The British Government gave the go-ahead for the Battle of Passchendaele – in which some 400,000 soldiers were killed or wounded – primarily to sustain French morale. *See p. 59.*

7 There were probably real possibilities for a negotiated peace in the winter of 1917/18, which Britain helped to sabotage. *See pp. 57–59.*

8 Britain might have gone over the precipice into fascism had the war continued much longer. *See pp. 65–68.*

9 Britain 'recruited' over a million African 'carriers' during the war, at least 95,000 of whom were worked to death or died from disease. *See p. 79.*

10 A Maori princess led one of the most successful examples of communal resistance to the war. *See pp. 74–78.*

1   YouGov Polls, 9–10 July 2013 and 7–8 January 2014; 'Do Mention the War: Will 1914 Matter in 2014?', *British Future*, 2013, p. 2.

2   David French, *The Strategy of the Lloyd George Coalition, 1916–1918*, Oxford University Press, 1995, p. 3.

Introduction

A celebration of the people and movements that opposed the First World War

This project has its origins in Adam Hochschild's book *To End All Wars* which is a window into the world of anti-war activists at the beginning of the twentieth century. When Gabriel and I read it we were very excited by their lives and stories – they felt very close. Before reading this book the image of the war resisters in our vague subconscious was probably something worthy, rather dull and earnestly noble. We discovered that our imaginings were very wrong. What we were immediately struck by was these people's creativity and mischievousness, their strategic planning and effective mass organising.

Despite having both spent our adult lives in anti-war movements we had a quite limited knowledge of what was done to resist 'The Great War for Civilisation' beyond the important contribution of the conscientious objectors. And it was apparent that the characters that Adam Hochschild had given us were not likely to be commemorated within the official framework of a Festival of Remembrance: a tradition which presents the 'heroism' of the men who followed orders as a uniquely noble form of self sacrifice.

Rosziska
Schwimmer

"What is needed," we thought, "is to create some cultural self-defence against this government's use of First World War history to bolster present political commitments to militarism and armaments. What is needed is a People's History! Gabriel will dig out more of these stories from the hinterlands of history; I will make posters of them; and we'll commission poems and songs from Mererid Hopwood, Alan Brownjohn, Dan Kennedy, Anna Robinson and Krysia Mansfield, so that we can all sing these lives into the present. We can use this opportunity to celebrate the sanity and ferocious commitment, the humour and stubbornness, the great numbers and far-reach of our anti-war forebears. We will commemorate self-sacrifice for the ideals of internationalism, feminism, pacifism, anarchism, socialism and love of humanity."

Millions of people across the world resisted co-option into the war machine in one way or another, and our tiny selection has been made to give a taste of the lesser known characters, incidents and movements. Where we have focused on Britain we have attempted to show the wider political context in which the anti-war activities were taking place: the campaigns for suffrage and the labour movement, feminist analysis and anti-imperialism. And where we step off British shores to look for representatives of resistance on the Continent, our two stories are about German men; these we use to highlight the revolutionary struggles in Europe and also how the politics of the War facilitated the slaughter of civilian populations, most notably in the Armenian Genocide.

We begin with a look at the backstory of the European imperial powers and place the Great War within a continuum of a world war that had been going on for centuries. Despite the prefix 'World', the impact of the 'First World War' on the Global South is presently just a glimmer in our national consciousness and the overwhelming concern is the European experience of the war. It was therefore very important to us to find the actual names of war resisters in the Global South: this has been like chasing photons. Gabriel chased long and hard through libraries and archives around the world to catch names and tales from Africa, the Ottoman Empire and the Antipodes. The minutiae of this research, including new material you won't find in this little book, can be found fully referenced on *The World is My Country* website.

The process of bringing together these stories has given us many moments of frisson that must be familiar to historians: time collapsing between the stacks in Kings College Library as we read through copies of the *Tribunal* and laughed at the jokes of a hundred years ago; immersing ourselves in 1916 as we traced Bertrand Russell's appearances in mining towns through scanned newspapers in the National Library of Wales; looking at Armin Wegner's photographs and turning away and attempting to look again through time and see the once-lived lives of the corpses of loved people. And there were also connections between the present and the past. I found myself simultaneously working on the Alice Wheeldon image and on a linocut

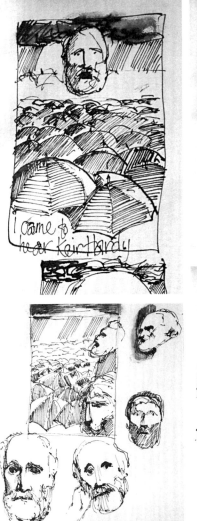

I came to
hear Keir Hardy

AUGUST 2ᴺᴰ 1914

I came to hear
Keir Hardy

Stand firm Rata

Grandfather
King Tawhiao 1881

for 'Police Spies Out of Lives' (a contemporary pressure group to get justice for women who had unknowingly had relationships with undercover police officers who used them as surveillance cover): women on either side of a century who were open hearted. The serpents that poisoned those lives entered both of my images.

It seemed fitting that we name the whole project after a closing line from Alice Wheeldon's prison letters:

'Thine in the courage of internationalism,
the world is my country, is it thine?'.

The stories that follow each stand alone; we invite you to peruse them in any order. Get copies of the posters, poems and songs from the *Peace News* webshop, distribute them, change history.

Then change the future.

Emily Johns

www.theworldismycountry.info

www.peacenews.info

Nsala sits with the hand and foot of his five-year-old daughter, Boali, 1904.
The systematic cutting off of hands by Belgian colonists and their proxies was widely practiced in
King Leopold's Congo. Photograph by Alice Seeley Harris.

Other People's Freedoms

Winston Churchill, January 1914:
We have got all we want in territory, and our claim to be left in the unmolested enjoyment of vast and splendid possessions, mainly acquired by violence, largely maintained by force, often seems less reasonable to others than to us.[1]

In his 2014 prime time apologia for the First World War, Max Hastings argued that the conflict was 'tragically necessary' because 'the people in Germany cared nothing for democracy or other people's freedoms'.[2]

In reality, British, French, Russian, Italian and US elites also 'cared nothing for democracy or other people's freedoms'. Indeed, occupation, massacre and imperial exploitation were commonplace pre-war, and continued without a pause once the war was over.[3]

They were also actively opposed by many of those who resisted the First World War.

The *First* World War?

The very term 'The First World War' is highly ideological. Viewed from the Global South there was already a 'world war' in progress on 27 June 1914: namely, a war by the European (and American) empires against much of the rest of the world.

Indeed, '[b]etween 1800 and 1914 the proportion of the earth's surface occupied by Europeans, whether in colonies or former colonies, rose from

35 to 84.4 per cent'[4] – and the process whereby this happened was very far from peaceful.

Plucky Little Belgium

German atrocities in the pre-war period were real enough. Scores of thousands of people were killed in German South-West Africa (today's Namibia), in what was probably the 20th century's first genocide.

However, Hastings' claim that this genocide was 'worse than any British excess' is disingenuous.[5] For, in absolute terms, it paled before Belgium's genocidal depredations in King Leopold's 'Congo Free State', where murder, starvation, disease and a plummeting birth-rate cut the population by half – some ten million people – between 1880 and 1920.[6]

Interested only in drawing parallels between the Kaiser's Germany and the Nazis, Hastings passes over this inconvenient fact in silence.

Other people's crises

No account of the origins of the First World War is complete without references to the 'Morocco Crises' of 1905 and 1911 – two *diplomatic* crises involving France and Germany. But how many know that in August 1907, France shelled Casablanca, killing so many people that the stench from the corpses made the air 'foetid a mile off the coast'?[7]

Similarly, Russia repeatedly intervened, with British backing, to crush Iran's constitutional revolution in the years leading up to the war, using artillery to mow down 'every living creature in the streets' of Tabriz[8], while Italy invaded Libya, massacring thousands, and the brutal US counterinsurgency war in the Philippines claimed the lives of over half-a-million Filipinos.

Murdering natives, stealing lands

Britain's record – if honestly faced – is just as grim, if not grimmer.

For example, in 1898, British forces led by Lord Kitchener used machine-guns to mow down over 10,000 Sudanese in a single day, coming precipitously close to starting a war with France; British losses totalled 48.[9]

And, in terms of numbers, few events can match the 'Late Victorian Holocausts' that occurred in the 19th century as millions of Indians, Chinese and Brazilians were 'forcibly incorporated' into the political and economic structures of a London-centred world economy, and then 'murdered by the application of utilitarian free trade principles' during three global El Niño droughts.[10]

Still far from over

In 1911, German socialist Rosa Luxemburg – later interned during the war as a threat to the state – noted that if the Europeans were serious about peace, 'they would give up their colonies and end their policy of carving out spheres of influence throughout the world.'[11] Over a century later, the world-war-before-the-First-World-War is still far from over.[12] So is the need for those in the imperial heartlands to speak out and to resist.

1 Emphasis added. The quote is from a secret memo Churchill wrote as First Lord of the Admiralty. When he published these remarks a decade later he deleted the emphasised words (Jean Bricmont & Julie Franck (eds), *Chomsky Notebook*, Columbia University Press, 2007, pp. 44–45).

2 'The Necessary War', BBC2, first broadcast 25 February 2014.

3 E.g., in 1920 British planes killed and wounded an estimated 8,450 Iraqis (Nicholson Baker, *Human Smoke*, Simon and Schuster, 2008, p. 8).

4 David Stevenson, *1914–1918*, Penguin, 2005, p. 6.

5 As note 2. above. Hastings also fails to mention that Britain was complicit in the genocide, providing trade supplies to the Germans via South Africa as it was taking place (Heather Jones, 'The German Empire', p. 61 in Robert Gerwarth & Erez Manela (eds), *Empires at War: 1911–1923*, Oxford University Press, 2014).

6 Adam Hochschild, *King Leopold's Ghost*, Papermac, 2000, pp. 226, 233.

7 'The Casablanca Outrage', *Taranaki Herald*, 13 August 1907.

8 'The Tabriz Massacre', *Wanganui Chronicle*, 28 December 1911.

9 Adam Hochschild, *To End All Wars*, MacMillan, 2011, p. 18; Sven Lindqvist, *Exterminate All the Brutes*, Granta, 1996, p. 67.

10 Mike Davis, *The Origins of the Third World*, Corner House Briefing #27, December 2002, p. 29.

11 Harry Harmer, *Rosa Luxemburg*, Haus, 2008, pp. 83–84.

12 For surveys of US and British actions in the post-WW2 period see William Blum, *Killing Hope*, Zed, 2014 and Mark Curtis, *Unpeople*, Vintage, 2004. According to Curtis, 'Britain bears significant responsibility for around 10 million deaths since 1945... including Nigerians, Indonesians, Arabians, Ugandans, Chileans, Vietnamese and many others.' (*ibid.*, p.2)

An evitable war[1]

First Lord of the Admiralty, Winston Churchill, 28 July 1914: *Everything tends toward catastrophe & collapse. I am interested, geared up and happy.*[2]

The First World War was not inevitable. Firstly, because an Anglo-German war was far from fated. Secondly, because, even during the 'July crisis' of 1914 that led to the war, there were (untaken) opportunities to prevent it. And thirdly, because Britain – whose participation was probably decisive in prolonging the conflict and turning it into a global war – did not *have* to intervene at all.

The wars that didn't happen

Because the First and Second World Wars both pitted Germany against France, Britain, the US and Russia, these alignments have come to seem foreordained. In fact, '[i]n the years before 1914, there could have been a war over colonial issues between Britain and the United States, Britain and France, or Britain and Russia – and in each case there nearly was.'[3]

Moreover, it cannot 'be claimed that there were insuperable forces generating an ultimately lethal Anglo-German antagonism': around the turn of the century an Anglo-German understanding 'seemed not only desirable but possible' to statesmen in both countries.[4]

Paths not taken

War remained evitable once the July crisis had begun.

For example, the British Government could have conducted – and peace activists pushed for – 'a credible, active diplomacy of mediation – strengthened by a commitment to strict neutrality and genuinely even-handed negotiation'.[5] It didn't.

Instead, Britain made a series of provocative moves that compromised its ability to mediate[6], while at the same time doing 'very little to restrain… Russia', whose 'impatience to mobilise' was a key factor in the crisis.[7]

Britain also rejected a series of German offers to exchange a British pledge of neutrality for German commitments: to make no annexations in Europe; to guarantee the integrity of France and her colonies; to respect Belgian neutrality; and not to use her naval forces against France's northern coast.[8] It also rejected a German attempt to confine the war to Eastern Europe.[9]

Enormous changes at the last minute

The possibilities for averting disaster should not be underestimated.

On 1 August 1914, 'even the whiff of a continuing possibility of British neutrality' led the German Emperor 'to demand sweeping changes in the German war plan', exasperating his generals and temporarily sparing both Belgium and France from invasion.[10]

What might have happened had Britain exerted itself for peace?

1 evitable: capable of being avoided (Merriam-Webster).

2 Douglas Newton, *Darkest Days*, Verso, 2014, p. 51. Churchill did his best to frogmarch events in the direction of war – see note 6. below and *ibid.*, pp. 50–54, 132. On 22 February 1915, Churchill told Asquith's daughter Violet: 'I think a curse should rest on me – because I *love* this war. I know it's smashing & shattering the lives of thousands every moment – & yet – I *can't* help it – I enjoy every second of it' (Niall Ferguson, *The Pity of War*, Penguin, 1998, pp. 177–178, emphasis in original).

3 Margaret MacMillan, *The War that Ended Peace*, Profile Books, 2014, p. 55.

4 Ferguson, *op. cit.*, pp. 45–46, 49. Concealed from the public, one of Britain's 'two reasons' for fighting was 'to secure a peace settlement which would enhance the security of Britain and its empire against not just its enemies, but also against its allies' (David French, *The Strategy of the Lloyd George Coalition, 1916–1918*, p. 3). Indeed, British policy makers originally planned to let the other Great Powers – allies and enemies alike – bleed each other dry so that an essentially unbloodied Britain could then step in and 'grasp the lion's share of the spoils… dictat[ing] terms not just to their enemies but also to their allies' (*ibid.*, p. 4).

5 Newton, *op. cit.*, p. 300.

6 E.g. Churchill encouraged the advocates of 'firmness' in Russia and France by first ordering the British First Fleet not to disperse after a test mobilisation and then publicising this initiative to the press (*ibid.*, pp. xx, 27–30).

7 *Ibid.*, pp. 27–29, 300; MacMillan, *op. cit.*, pp. xxxi.

8 Newton, *op. cit.*, pp. 84, 141, 221, 357 n.23.

9 *Ibid.*, p. 150.

10 *Ibid.*, p. 152.

War Against War

Keir Hardie, 2 August 1914:
We are here to say that, so far as we can decree, there shall be no shot fired, no sabre drawn in this war of conquest. The only class which can prevent the Government going to war is the working class.[1]

When the heavens opened up half an hour into the rally 'the solid core… stood gallantly to their umbrellas and cheered for the war against war'.[2]

Standing on the plinth at the base of Nelson's Column, labour activist Keir Hardie began his speech by reminding the 15,000-strong crowd of the murder of the French socialist leader Jean Jaurès two days earlier.[3]

With Jaurès' support, Hardie had spent the past four years trying to get the Second International – the international organisation of socialist and labour parties – to agree a plan for a simultaneous international strike 'on the first rumour of war'.[4] But progress had been glacial, and now Jaurès was dead, killed by a fanatical nationalist.

'We shall have no great anti-war campaign by the Liberals', Hardie

2nd AUGUST 1914

Government going to war is the

The only class which can prevent the
working class

told the crowd. 'The church will not lead in this holy war against crime and bloodshed. The task is left to the workers.' [5]

Two days later Britain declared war on Germany. Hardie's hope that the threat of international working-class solidarity could stop the conflict was finally destroyed and he 'found it increasingly difficult to sustain any viable line of criticism against the war, so apparently overwhelming was the national support for the government' in the war's early months.[6]

But other, younger, activists were waiting in the wings.

A 'very, very radical feminist' [7]

Recently appointed as the press secretary of the 26-nation International Women's Suffrage Alliance (IWSA), the 36-year-old Hungarian feminist Rosika Schwimmer was present on 4 August as Big Ben struck midnight and the surrounding crowd began to shout 'War is declared!'.[8]

Returning home, she penned an open letter calling for the formation of an 'International Watching Committee' of representatives from the neutral governments, that would send daily mediation offers to the warring parties.

Resigning from her job she sent messages to all of the IWSA's national sections, receiving positive responses from France, Germany, Hungary, Holland, Sweden and Norway. Forced to sell her jewellery and typewriter in order to remain solvent, she 'even tried to sell her clothes in order to be able to telegraph more contacts in European countries'.[9]

Travelling to the US, she met with President Wilson, and embarked on a US tour, '[s]peaking three to six times a day, not only in public halls but on street corners and at factory gates'.[10] At the end of every speech she would urge her audience 'to send a resolution – a copy of which was on every seat – to [Wilson] insisting that he demand immediate cessation of hostilities'.[11]

In 1915 she played a decisive role in getting the International Women's Congress at the Hague to mandate a group of delegates to take its resolutions – which included a variant of Schwimmer's mediation idea – in person to the heads of the belligerent and neutral governments, and led the delegation to the neutrals.

Returning to the US, she orchestrated a campaign that resulted in Wilson receiving 12,000 telegrams in 3 days, demanding that he start a conference of neutrals. She then played a pivotal role in Henry Ford's ill-fated 'Peace Ship' before finally collapsing.

Persecuted by both communists and fascists during Hungary's post-war political turmoil, Schwimmer returned to the US in 1921, only to find herself a victim of the Red Scare.

Denied US citizenship because of her pacifism she became, in her own words, 'a woman without a country'.[12]

Nonetheless, she remained 'unshakeably committed to her ideals', writing, shortly before her death, that 'we sought equality for our half of the human race, not at the lowest, but at the highest level of human aspirations'.[13]

1 Douglas Newton, *Darkest Days* [hereafter 'Newton I'], 1914, Verso, 2014, p. 169.

2 *Manchester Guardian* quoted in Newton I, p. 170. 'War Against War' was the headline in an ad for the demo that appeared in the *Times* the day before (*ibid.*, p. 165).

3 Across Britain, probably over 100,000 Socialists and Labour supporters demonstrated against the looming war that Sunday afternoon, 2 August 1914 (David Boulton, *Objection Overruled*, MacGibbon & Kee, 1967, p. 33).

4 Douglas Newton, *British Labour, European Socialism and the Struggle for Peace, 1889–1914*, Oxford University Press, 1985, p. 256. The words quoted are from a proposal drafted by Hardie's Independent Labour Party in May 1910, for submission to a Congress of the International.

5 Newton I, p. 169.

6 Kenneth O. Morgan, *Keir Hardie*, Weidenfeld & Nicholson, 1984, p. 268.

7 Schwimmer's self-description (Anne Wiltsher, *Most Dangerous Women*, Pandora, 1985, p.10).

8 Schwimmer was also at the 2 August rally (*ibid.*, pp. 18–19).

9 *Ibid.*, pp. 31–32.

10 *Ibid.*, p. 46.

11 *Ibid.* By December 1914 she had spoken in at least 60 cities in 22 states.

12 Beth S. Wenger, 'Radical Politics in a Reactionary Age: The Unmaking of Rosika Schwimmer, 1914–1930' in *Journal of Women's History*, 1990, vol. 2, no. 2, p. 88.

13 *Ibid.*, p. 91; 'We must not fail in our pledge to end war', *Peace News*, 23 July 1948.

Embracing War

Arthur Henderson:
If being secretary of the Labour Party is in any way to preclude me from doing my duty to my country... I cho[ose] my country before my party.[1]

Before Britain's declaration of war on 4 August 1914, public support for the war was far from overwhelming.[2] However, '[b]y the end of 1914 the populations of England, Scotland, Wales and Ireland had largely embraced the war'[3], and this was true even of the war's most likely opponents.

Thus the Labour Party and the trade unions both swiftly backed the war, and even in the Independent Labour Party (ILP) – one of the only two large socialist parties in Europe to oppose the war once it had begun – dissenters were in a minority in 1914, and remained so until at least mid-1917.[4]

In a similar vein, the leaders of the Women's Social and Political Union (WSPU), Emmeline and Christabel Pankhurst, both became

On 25 May 1916, Clara Cole and Rosa Hobhouse were both sentenced to three months imprisonment for 'spreading false reports, by word and pamphlets, likely to prejudice recruiting'. The pair had been arrested in Kettering on day five of a 'peace pilgrimage' through Bedfordshire and Northamptonshire. Dressed as nuns, they had been distributing anti-war literature along the way, including a pamphlet stating: 'Don't you think it is a shame that young fellows should go on killing one another for the sake of a few rulers'.[11]

In 1916, the following passage from a flier entitled 'Negotiations', by Charles Buxton, was deemed to be in contravention of the Defence of the Realm Act: 'In urging Negotiation, we should give much-needed support to the section of the Cabinet which is said to favour this course.' [12]

Manchester's first woman Councillor, Margaret Ashton, was threatened with prosecution for advising the citizens of Warrington not to buy War Bonds. As a result of her peace activism, the Council passed a resolution after the war 'labell[ing] her as a friend of the enemy' and refused to hang a portrait of her that the Guardian's editor had commissioned to celebrate Ashton's 70th birthday. [13]

rabidly pro-war[5] – organising a vast pro-war rally in Whitehall, funded by the government[6], and touring the country to speak at recruitment meetings. [7]

Almost all of the British churches threw themselves into the war effort, as both a national and an ethical duty, and even the Quakers were divided: by 1917 an estimated one-third of military-age Quakers had enlisted. [8]

Meanwhile, the state had a wide range of repressive powers at its disposal for dealing with dissent – ranging from banning meetings and pre-emptive arrest, to restricting people's movements and opening their mail[9] – and could also rely upon the support of elite-sponsored patriotic mobs and the collaboration of the mainstream media, as well as its own substantial propaganda resources. [10]

All in all, therefore, opponents of the war had a steep hill to climb.

1 Brock Millman, *Managing Domestic Dissent in First World War Britain*, Frank Cass, 2000, p. 12.

2 Douglas Newton, *Darkest Days*, 2014, Verso, 2014, p. 175.

3 Catriona Pennell, *A Kingdom United*, Oxford University Press, 2014, p. 1.

4 Millman, *op. cit.*, p. 11.

5 In December 1915 the WSPU's paper (now renamed 'Britannia') was seized for a libellous attack on the foreign secretary, having claimed that '[t]he cold, premeditated long-calculated treachery of Sir Edward Grey might, indeed almost make Judas of old time blush'. The next issue – which had to be printed using a hand-worked duplicating machine, the Government having warned-off potential publishers – declared 'BRITANNIA RECANTS NOTHING AND REITERATES EVERYTHING' (Millman, *op. cit.*, pp. 42, 120).

6 The WSPU received a £2,000 grant from the Ministry of Munitions to finance a parade asserting 'women's right to serve' (Andrew Rosen, *Rise Up, Women!*, Routledge, 2013, p. 252).

7 The executive of the non-militant National Union of Women's Suffrage Societies split 'exactly in two' over the war, with the anti-war women resigning (Ann Wiltsher, *Most Dangerous Women*, Pandora, 1985, p. 77).

8 Margaret Hirst, *The Quakers on War and Peace*, Swarthmore Press, 1923, Appendix F, p. 538.

9 Millman, *op. cit.*, pp. 254, 170, 82, 183.

10 See pp. 65–68 of this booklet.

11 E. Sylvia Pankhurst, *The Home Front*, The Cresset Library, 1987, p. 329; 'Women Peace Cranks: £50 fines for trying to stop recruiting', *Feilding Star*, 19 July 1916.

12 'Seditious Propaganda', Bundle 2, HO/139/23, Public Record Office.

13 Wiltsher, *op. cit.*, p. 197; 'Who was Margaret Ashton?', BBC Manchester, 4 July 2006.

Skeffy

Francis Sheehy-Skeffington, 9 June 1915:
If you condemn me, you condemn the system you represent... Any sentence you may pass on me is a sentence upon British rule in Ireland.[1]

Sentenced to six months hard labour the small red-bearded gentleman wearing the 'Votes for Women' badge had been defiant. To loud cheering from the public gallery he had declared: 'I will serve no such sentence. I will eat no food from this moment, and long before the expiration of the sentence I shall be out of prison, alive or dead!'

Seven days later, a pale skeleton of his recent self, he was released under the Cat and Mouse Act. He was never recalled to complete his sentence.

The year was 1915, the place Dublin, and the name of the gentleman with the beard and badge, jailed for speaking out against the war, was Francis Sheehy-Skeffington.

'A small instrument that makes revolutions'
Writing in 1916, James Stephens noted that Sheehy-Skeffington had 'been in every trouble that has touched Ireland these ten years back... [always] on the generous side'.[2]

THE
IRISH CITIZEN
AUGUST 15, 1914. – ONE PENNY
VOTES FOR WOMEN
NOW!
DAMN
YOUR WAR!

FRANCIS SHEEHY SKEFFINGTON

A vegetarian, anti-vivisectionist, anti-clerical, teetotaller and nonsmoker, his life was dominated by four causes: feminism, pacifism, socialism and Irish nationalism.[3] To those who branded him a crank he would respond: 'Yes, that's right, and a crank is a small instrument that makes revolutions.'

'Branches of the same tree'

His wife Hanna co-founded the Irish Women's Franchise League (IWFL), the militant wing of the Irish suffrage movement, and Francis edited the League's newspaper, the *Irish Citizen.*

Skeffington viewed war and anti-feminism as 'branches of the same tree – disregard of true life-values'. It is therefore unsurprising that less than a fortnight after Britain's declaration of war, the *Citizen* produced a poster bearing the immortal slogan: 'Votes for Women Now! Damn Your War!'

Beresford Place

In the Autumn of 1914 he began speaking out against the war every Sunday at Beresford Place in Dublin, 'standing in a little niche of stone under the railway bridge at the Custom House, close to Liberty Hall'. [4]

Despite the fact that the country was on the brink of civil war at the conflagration's outset, large numbers of Irishmen from both north and south enlisted. Undeterred, Skeffington continued to speak out every Sunday.

In all he would deliver 40 such speeches, 'analysing in logical fashion the war situation' [5], until he was arrested on 29 May 1915 for 'mak[ing] statements... likely to prejudice recruiting for His Majesty's Forces'.

Nonviolent revolution

Not just a practitioner of active nonviolence, he also advocated nonviolent revolution, criticising the militarism of the (armed) Irish Volunteers, asking:

'Can you not conceive of... an organisation of people prepared to dare all things for their object, prepared to suffer and to die rather than abandon one jot of their principles – but an organisation that will not lay it down as its fundamental principle: 'We will prepare to kill our fellow men'?'

Death & vindication

Skeffington was detained by the British military during the 1916 Easter Rising and summarily executed. Two days before his death he had braved a hail of bullets to try to rescue a wounded British soldier, explaining: 'I could not let anyone bleed to death while I could help.'

Though he did not live to see the many causes that he espoused succeed, had he lived just another 26 months he would at least have seen some of his claims concerning conscription and civil resistance partially vindicated.

The attempt to introduce conscription in Ireland in 1918 led to a general strike that brought 'virtually the whole of Ireland to a standstill', forcing the Government to back down.[6]

1 Leah Levenson, *With Wooden Sword*, Northeastern University Press, 1983, p. 177. Unless otherwise sourced, all Sheehy-Skeffington quotes are taken from this book.

2 James Stephens, *The Insurrection in Dublin*, Colm Smyth Ltd, 1992, p. 50.

3 According to Roger McHugh, during their honeymoon Francis and Hanna visited one of her favourite uncles, who had been warned off drinking alcohol by his doctor. Discovering a full bottle of whiskey on the premises, Francis proceeded to pour it down the sink, declaring that 'he would do everything possible to prevent her uncle's death'. 'Her uncle carried this preventive logic a stage further by showing them both out'. (Roger McHugh, 'Thomas Kettle and Francis Sheehy-Skeffington', pp. 132-133 in Conor Cruise O'Brien (ed.), *The Shaping of Modern Ireland*, Routledge and Keegan Paul, 1960).

4 Hanna Sheehy-Skeffington, 'An Irish Pacifist', pp. 340–341 in Julian Bell (ed), *We Did Not Fight. 1914–1918 experiences of war resisters*, Cobden-Sanderson, 1935.

5 *Ibid.*

6 Liz Curtis, *The Cause of Ireland*, Beyond the Pale Publications, 1984, pp. 300–301. The shelving of the plans did not produce a state of quiescence. On 9 July 1918 the Defence of the Realm Act was used to ban 'all meetings and processions in public places in the whole of Ireland. Concerts, hurling matches, and literary competitions were suppressed.' In response '1,500 hurling matches were played on 4 August, and on 15 August hundreds of public meetings were held, with speakers being jailed as a result.'

Over 500 political arrests were made between mid-May and mid-December. (*ibid.*, p. 302).

Armin T. Wegner, 1915–1916

**Armin Wegner, Aleppo,
19 October 1916:**
*I have taken numerous photographs
during the past few days... I have
no doubt that I am committing high
treason...*[1]

Along with several other officers, he had
risked a possible death sentence by taking
the pictures in the first place. Now, returning
to Germany with the 'images of horror and accusation' rolled into a
bundle against his stomach to prevent their detection by the authorities,
he was determined to do whatever he could for the victims.[1]

The year was 1916, and the name of the thirty-year-old soldier was
Armin T. Wegner.

Today, these photographs form 'the core of the witness images' of the
single worst atrocity of the First World War: the Armenian genocide
– the centrally planned campaign of 'annihilation' by the Ottoman
authorities that killed over a million people.[2]

'A thousand pleading hands'

More than a million Armenians were deported from their homes during
the genocide and, as part of Field Marshal von der Goltz's retinue,

Wegner encountered their death marches as he travelled across Anatolia on the way to Baghdad.

'The roads are lined with the famished and suffering Armenian refugees,' he wrote, 'like a weeping hedge that begs and screams, and from which rise a thousand pleading hands.'[3]

Unable to remain a bystander, Wegner defied orders and entered the deportees' makeshift camps. He took scores of photographs there – a capital crime – and wrote letters about the genocide, one of which was published in 1916 in his mother's feminist magazine *Die Frau der Gegenwart*.

During a brief period of home leave, he contacted the editor of the Berlin newspaper *Die Welt am Montag*, in an unsuccessful attempt to raise awareness about the genocide. Around the world the press devoted substantial coverage to the topic. But in Germany it was *verboten*.[4]

Arrested

Back on Ottoman territory, he was arrested by German soldiers and put to work in a cholera unit in Baghdad, where the senior hospital doctor was instructed that Wegner should 'be utilized in such a way so as to do away with any desire [of his]… to wander around' the city.[5]

Later, travelling back to Istanbul, he visited still more camps and took more photographs.

After the war he wrote an 'open letter' about the genocide that was reproduced in the daily newspaper *Berliner Tageblatt*, published four

books on the topic, and lectured publicly about it 'despite frequent rioting by Turkophile groups during his talks'.[6] In 1934, after being tortured by the Nazis, he fled Germany and spent most of his remaining 44 years in exile.

'I am not a bandit'

Turkish civilians also disobeyed orders in resistance to the Armenian genocide.

For example, the governor of Ankara, Mazhar Bey, pretended not to understand the written orders he had been sent regarding the deportations. When a government official was sent to relay the orders to him directly, he told him:

'No, Atıf Bey, I am the governor, I'm not a bandit. I cannot do it. I will get up from th[e governor's] chair and you can come and do it.'[7]

The courage to disobey

Arguably, 'Wars happen not because as a species we have a tendency towards physical aggression, but because we have a tendency towards obedience to authority. We obey too much and resist too little.'[8]

During these centenary years, there will be no shortage of voices encouraging us to remember – and celebrate – the 'heroism' of the men who followed orders. With good reason, we choose instead to celebrate those, like Armin Wegner and Mazhar Bey, who exercised true moral courage, thought for themselves and chose to disobey.

1 Sybil Milton, 'Armin T. Wegner, Polemicist for Armenian and Jewish Human Rights', *Journal of Armenian Studies*, 1992, Vol. IV, p. 168.

2 Peter Balakian, *The Burning Tigris*, Harper Collins, 2003, pp. 258-59. 'In a report dated 30 June 1915, German consul general Mordtmann recounts to his superiors a conversation with Ottoman interior minister Talat Pasha... Regarding the deportation, Talat told him "what we are talking about here... is the annihilation of the Armenians"' (Taner Akçam, *The Young Turks' Crime Against Humanity*, Princeton University Press, 2013, pp. 201-202).

3 Letter dated 26 November 1915, *Armin T. Wegner and the Armenians in Anatolia, 1915: Images and Testimonies* [hereafter 'Images'], Guerni E Associati, 1996, p. 61.

4 Newspaper editor Hellmut Gerlach would later write that: 'Official censorship sealed our lips. During a press conference, we were told it was "undesirable" for us to talk about the persecution of the Armenians.' (*Images*, pp. 49–50).

5 Johanna Wernicke-Rothmayer, *Armin T. Wegner: Gesellschaftserfahrung und literarisches Werk*, p. 33.

6 Martin Rooney, 'A forgotten humanist: Armin T. Wegner', *Journal of Genocide Research*, 2000, pp. 117–118.

7 Akçam, *op. cit.*, p. 195. Hüseyin Nesimî, the senior administrator of Lice County, 'refused to carry out the order to massacre his Armenian residents'. Having 'first demanded to receive a written order to this effect... he was removed from his position, summoned to Diyarbekır, and murdered en route' (*ibid.*, p. 196).

8 Milan Rai, 'Deadly Obedience', *Peace News*, March 2011, http://peacenews.info/node/3856/deadly-obedience.

The Banning of Bertie

Bertrand Russell:
Several Red Tabs... besought me to acquire a sense of humour... afterwards I regretted that I had not replied that I held my sides with laughter every morning as I read the casualty figures.[1]

The publicity from his trial had undoubtedly helped to bring people out. At Briton Ferry the hall had been packed – and a resolution in favour of immediate peace negotiations had been carried unanimously – while at Port Talbot a crowd of 400 'listened with the closest attention'.[2] Here at least, the new Allied offensive on the Somme had not rallied people around the flag.

In Cardiff on 6 July 1916 – day six of his 24-day speaking tour – there had been some opposition. However, apart from the 'blood-thirsty middle-aged man' who had claimed to be a soldier and 'spoiled his case by violence', they had not caused any problems.[3]

During the following week, as a result of the trial, he was dismissed from his job at Trinity College Cambridge, and received a letter from Harvard telling him that he had been denied a passport. Finally, on 1 September 1916, his Cardiff speech being cited as the pretext, Bertrand Russell, England's greatest living philosopher, was banned from 'an area constituting one-third of [Britain]'.[4]

THE BANNING OF BERTIE
BRITAIN'S GREATEST LIVING PHILOSOPHER
BERTRAND RUSSELL WAS BANNED UNDER THE
DEFENCE OF THE REALM ACT FROM A THIRD
OF THE COUNTRY FOR AN ANTI-WAR
SPEECH HE MADE IN CARDIFF
ON 6TH JULY 1916

'All this madness'

In a letter to the *Nation*, published on 15 August 1914, he had written:

'All this madness, all this rage, all this flaming death of our civilisation and our hopes, has been brought about because a set of official gentlemen, living luxurious lives, mostly stupid, and all without imagination or heart, have chosen that it should occur rather than that any one of them should suffer some infinitesimal rebuff to his country's pride.'[5]

On 5 June 1916, he was found guilty of 'making statements likely to prejudice... recruiting', after declaring his authorship of a leaflet entitled 'Two Years' Hard Labour for Refusing to Disobey the Dictates of Conscience'.[6]

The trial delayed his tour of South Wales, where he gave about 35 anti-war talks.[7]

The 'blood-thirsty' audience member in Cardiff was Captain Atherley Jones, the organising secretary of the far-right British Empire Union. He had stated that Russell 'ought to be locked up', but no official action was taken until Jones had a letter published in the *Daily Express* three weeks later, leading the Home Secretary to request a transcript of the speech.[8]

Prohibited areas

The banning order followed, prohibiting Russell from 'resid[ing] in or enter[ing]' any area designated 'prohibited' under the Aliens Restrictions Act 1914.[9]

Four days after receiving it Russell met with General George Cockerill at the War Office, the latter offering to lift the ban if Russell would abandon politics and return to mathematics.[10] Russell refused.

So indignant was Russell at Cockerill's suggestion that there might be 'some lack of a sense of humour in going on reiterating the same thing', that for the rest of his life 'he refused… to lay claim to the quality', later writing:

'I gathered that if I had had my proper share of the sense of the ludicrous, I should have been highly diverted at the thought of several thousand men a day being blown to bits, which I confess to my shame, never caused me even to smile'.[11]

The last laugh
Nonetheless, Russell still had the last laugh.

On 17 October 1916, the President of the Miners' Federation of Great Britain, Robert Smillie, departed from his usual practice by reading his talk at a thousand-strong protest meeting in Glasgow. After speaking for a considerable length of time, Smillie revealed to his audience that he was actually reading a lecture that the ban had prevented Russell from giving in person.

According to the *Glasgow Herald*: 'This announcement was received with laughter, followed by prolonged applause'.[12]

1 Bertrand Russell, *Autobiography*, Unwin, 1987, p. 262. A 'Red Tab' is a high-ranking officer in the British army.

2 Jo Vellacott, *Bertrand Russell and the Pacifists in the First World War*, Palgrave MacMillan, 1981, p. 87.

3 *Ibid.*, p. 88.

4 Bernd Frohmann, Mark Lippincott & Richard A. Rempel (eds), *The Collected Papers of Bertrand Russell, Volume 13*, Routledge, 2000, p. lxiv.

5 Russell, *op. cit.*, p. 265.

6 The No-Conscription Fellowship had distributed ½ million copies of the leaflet (Ray Monk, *Bertrand Russell: The Spirit of Solitude*, Vintage, 1997, p. 462). The timing of Russell's prosecution suggests that the Home Office may have decided to prosecute him under pressure from the Foreign Office, to create a pretext for denying him a passport (*ibid.*, p. 464).

7 His itinerary included: Port Talbot, Briton Ferry, Ystradgynlais, Cwmavon, Cardiff, Pontypridd, Merthyr Tydfil, Abercanaid, Pentrebâch, Troed-y-rhiw, Dowlais, Swansea, Pontypool, Bargoed, Abertillery, Newport, and Brynmawr (Frohmann et al, *op. cit.*, pp. lxxxviii–xc).

8 At the suggestion of the police, the chief reporter of the *Western Mail* had recorded Russell's speech in short-hand (Vellacott, *op. cit.*, p. 88).

9 Russell supposed that the ban had been imposed 'for fear that he would stir up labour unrest' (Frohmann et al, *op. cit.*, p. 453). The Government's real motive was to prevent him from keeping an appointment to meet COs engaged in 'alternative service' at a work camp in Suffolk. (Monk, *op. cit.*, pp. 472 -473).

10 Frohmann et al, *op. cit.*, p. 456.

11 *Ibid.*; Vellacott, *op. cit.*, p. 94.

12 *Ibid.*, p. 99.

The great case of Bodkin v. Bodkin

Archibald Bodkin: *This discussion seems to enable my learned friend to show his great sense of humour in the Court.*

R.C. Hawkin: *Humour does not occur here, except that this is the great case of Bodkin v. Bodkin, and I represent one side.*[1]

On 30 September 1916, peace activist Edward Fuller was prosecuted at Stratford Magistrates Court. His crime? Requesting a quote to have a poster, featuring the words of government lawyer Archibald Bodkin, exhibited in various parts of East London. The prosecutor's name? Archibald Bodkin.

The poster had been produced by the No-Conscription Fellowship (NCF). One of the main anti-war organisations in Britain during WWI, the NCF provided support to those refusing conscription, over 6,000 of whom were jailed, often under harsh conditions.

An unwitting 'pacifist speech'

Conscription became law in Britain in January 1916, and in May 1916 eight members of the NCF's national committee were convicted and fined £100 each for printing a leaflet calling for its repeal.

During the trial the prosecutor, Crown Advocate[2] Archibald Bodkin, read out a passage from this leaflet, and commented himself that: 'War will become impossible if all men were to have the view that war is wrong'.[3]

Believing that Bodkin had 'kindly provided us with such a terse and explicit phrase, expressing our view regarding war', the NCF mischievously turned Bodkin's unwitting 'pacifist speech' into a poster, and had copies printed by the National Labour Press.

'A quotation for exhibiting posters'

In late August 1916 Mr A.E. Abrahams, managing director of the Borough Theatre Billposting Company Ltd in Stratford, received a letter from Fuller requesting a quotation for exhibiting 50 or more copies of the poster 'on hoardings in Stratford, Forest Gate, Ilford, Leytonstone, Wanstead and Woodford'.

Abrahams wrote back with a quote, asking Fuller if he had 'received the consent of the War Office to have this bill exhibited', at the same time sending the poster to the War Office. Fuller replied that he had no doubts about the legality of exhibiting the poster, and that he was sure the War Office would confirm this.

Fuller was subsequently summonsed to appear in court for unlawfully attempting to make 'in print, statements liable to prejudice recruiting, discipline, and administration of his Majesty's forces' – an act prohibited by the draconian Defence of the Realm (Consolidation) Regulations.[4]

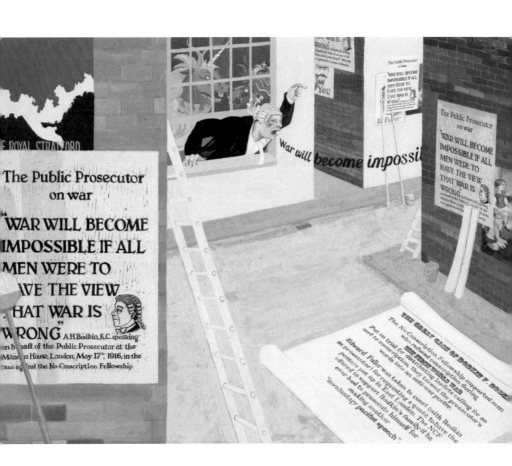

E ROYAL STRA**FORD**

The Public Prosecutor
on war

"WAR WILL BECOME
IMPOSSIBLE IF ALL
MEN WERE TO
AVE THE VIEW
HAT WAR IS
WRONG" A.H.Bodkin,K.C.speaking
on behalf of the Public Prosecutor at the
Mansion House, London, May 17th, 1916, in the
case against the No-Conscription Fellowship

War will become impossi

The Public Prosecutor
on war

WAR WILL BECOME
IMPOSSIBLE IF ALL
MEN WERE TO
HAVE THE VIEW
THAT WAR IS
WRONG.

THE GREAT CASE OF BODKIN V BODKIN

The No-Conscription Fellowship supported men
who refused conscription during WAR
Put on trial for distributing leaflets calling for an
end to conscription, they turned the prosecutor's
words into an anti-war poster.
Edward Fuller was taken to court to have the
prosecutor for requesting a quote to have the
posters put up in East London. The NCF
offered to support Bodkin's family if he
ever had to prosecute himself for
making another
"involuntary pacifist speech"

'It is a platitude'

During the trial, Bodkin called Brigadier-General B.E.W. Childs – then a senior military official from the War Office – to give his assessment of the likely impact of the poster on recruiting.

Cross-examined by Fuller's lawyer, R.C. Hawkin, Childs conceded that the statement was 'perfectly true' and 'a platitude'.

Nonetheless, Fuller was convicted and fined £100 – over £5,500 in today's money [5] – or 91 days imprisonment. Imprisoned, he was released before the sentence was fully served 'owing to Parliamentary protests on his behalf'. [6]

A vote of thanks

As a result of the case, the text of the Bodkin poster was widely reproduced verbatim in both the local and national press, including the *Daily Telegraph* and the *Weekly Dispatch* – reaching vastly more people than would ever have seen the original posters.

In its weekly newspaper, the *Tribunal*, the NCF noted, wryly, that: 'If, and when, Mr Bodkin himself is laid by the heels for uttering (unwittingly, of course, as heretofore) statements "likely to prejudice"…, etc., or if, it having again been brought to his notice that he has involuntarily made a pacifist speech, he decides in his devotion to duty to prosecute himself, then we promise to do all in our power to assist in the support of his dependants, should they be threatened with financial or other difficulty as a result of his persecution at the hands of the State or himself.' [7]

1 Edward Fuller and Dorothy Matthews, *Rex v. Edward Fuller: Report of Proceedings at Stratford Police Court, September 30, 1916, before Eliot Howard, Deputy-Lieutenant, and other Justices of the Becontree Hundred of Essex*, privately circulated, date unknown, p. 19. Unless otherwise sourced, all details about the case are drawn from this pamphlet.

2 The poster mistakenly refers to Bodkin as both 'The Public Prosecutor' and a K.C. (King's Counsel). As was conceded by Fuller's lawyer at the trial, neither description was correct.

3 Bodkin appears to have believed that he was merely restating the excerpt from the original leaflet. In fact the two statements had entirely different meanings: the original leaflet gave a *necessary* condition for war to become impossible (namely, that those men who didn't believe in war not fight); Bodkin's statement asserts a *sufficient* condition for war to become impossible (namely, for all men to come to the opinion that war is wrong).

4 Technically he was charged with having *prepared* to commit such an act. At least four other people were charged in relation to Bodkin's involuntary 'pacifist speech': Thomas John Williams of Pritchard Street, Tonyrefail (South Wales), his sister and two school-boys (*Tribunal*, 13 July 1916). Williams was charged 'with having under his control certain documents containing statements the publication of which would be likely to prejudice recruiting' – namely, copies of the NCF's newspaper, the *Tribunal*, that reproduced the Bodkin quote. His case was dismissed.

5 http://www.measuringworth.com/ukcompare/

6 E. Sylvia Pankhurst, *The Home Front*, The Cresset Library, 1987, p. 329.

7 'A Vote of Thanks', *Tribunal*, 5 October 1916.

Alice Wheeldon was a prophet

**Alice Wheeldon,
letter from prison:**
*Thine in the courage
of internationalism,
the world is my country,
is it thine?
God save the people.*

On 10 March 1917 Alice Wheeldon – a fifty-something seller of second-hand clothes, living in Derby – was sentenced to ten years imprisonment for allegedly conspiring to murder the Prime Minister, Lloyd George.

At her trial she was accused of scheming to have a dart, dipped in the Central American arrow poison curare, fired at the Prime Minister while he played golf on Walton Heath.

In less than a year she would be released from prison, never to return.

A 'shadowy informal network of resistance'
A feminist and a socialist, Alice made her living selling second-hand clothes from the front room of her house in Pear Tree Road. During

Alice Wheeldon ... was a prophet,

not of the sweet & holy
by e_____ by
_____ the
but of _____

_____ if ___ eldon could ____
___ back home
not with love and sympathy, but
_ intense hatred against _____
_ fills the world ___ warfare, ____
or crime, and all such ___ that

The World is my country

The
World
is my
Country

the war she became part of a 'shadowy informal network of resistance' that sheltered men who had gone on the run rather than be imprisoned for refusing to fight.[1]

Her daughters Hettie and Winnie were also active politically and her son William was a conscientious objector (CO).

Spies, lies and agents provocateurs

On 27 December 1916 a man calling himself Alex Gordon arrived on Alice's doorstep, claiming to be a CO on the run from the authorities. She sheltered him for the night and he introduced her to a second man, 'Comrade Bert'.

Unbeknownst to Alice the pair were actually agents for PMS2 – the intelligence unit of the Ministry of Munitions – who had been travelling about the country, encouraging socialists to engage in acts of sabotage and political violence.[2]

Within a few days of their first meeting, 'Gordon' – actually William Rickard, a mentally unstable man with a criminal background – had tricked Alice into asking Winnie to post her some poison, obtained from Winnie's husband Alfred Mason, a qualified pharmacist. The poison, Rickard claimed, was to be used to poison guard dogs at a prison camp for COs.

Prison and hunger strikes

On 30 January 1917, Alice, Hettie, Winnie and Alfred were all arrested and the poison cited as evidence of the alleged murder plot.

All but Hettie (who had wisely decided to have nothing to do with Rickard) were found guilty, in a trial that focussed as much on who the defendants were (atheists, pacifists, socialists) and what they believed, as on the alleged murder plot.[3]

In prison Alice began a series of hunger strikes, while on the outside mounting left-wing agitation over the case led to the closure of PMS2, whose functions were taken over by MI5.[4] By December 1917 Alice was close to death, and – frightened that she would die in prison and become a martyr – the authorities authorised her release on licence.[5]

'A prophet of the here and now'

Ostracised by her neighbours, Alice died in February 1919, a victim of the 'Spanish' flu pandemic.

The revolutionary lion-tamer John S. Clarke – on the run from the authorities as a war-resister – gave the funeral oration:

'Mrs Wheeldon was a socialist. She was a prophet, not of the sweet and holy by and by but of the here and now... If Mrs Wheeldon could speak, she would tell us to go back home not with love and sympathy, but with intense hatred against what fills the world with warfare, poverty or crime, and all such as that. She would tell us to go away to help bear the burden she has had to lay down... so as to obtain that glorious time when peace and joyousness shall fill all life.'[6]

Winnie Wheeldon's granddaughters are currently fighting a vigorous campaign to clear Alice's, Winnie's and Alfred's names.[7]

1 Sheila Rowbotham, *Friends of Alice Wheeldon*, Pluto Press, 1986, p. 116.

2 For example, in Salford Booth and Rickard suggested to British Socialist Party members that they should 'introduce bars of soap into engine boilers, salt into motor petrol tanks and bars of iron into machinery', spoke boldly of blowing up the House of Commons and urged one man to 'find the money to find the bombs to play hell'. (Nicholas Hiley, 'Internal Security in Wartime: The Rise and Fall of PMS2, 1915–1917', *Intelligence and National Security*, 1986, vol. 1, issue 3, p. 405).

3 Winnie Mason was sentenced to 5 years, Alfred Mason to 7 years. After the trial Rickard (who did not appear) was shipped off to South Africa where he 'performed a professional mesmerism act under the rather dramatic name "Vivid – the Magnetic Man"', before returning to England. (Nicola Rippon, *The Plot to Kill Lloyd George*, Wharncliffe Books, 2009, p. 154).

4 Hiley, *op. cit.*, pp. 408–410. In the same month that PMS2 was shut down, the Government decided to institute the 'systematic surveillance of the working class'. (Brock Millman, *Managing Dissent in First World War Britain*, Frank Cass, 2000, p. 179).

5 Documents at the National Archive suggest that the authorities may have intended to reimprison Alice under the 'Cat and Mouse Act' (brought in to counter the suffragette tactic of hunger strikes). However, '[t]he order signed eventually by a Home Secretary uncertain of his instructions did not admit the 1913 procedure.' (John Jackson, 'Losing the Plot: Lloyd George, F.E. Smith and the trial of Alice Wheeldon', *History Today*, May 2007, p. 46).

6 Rowbotham, *op. cit.*, pp. 83–84; Adam Hochschild, *To End All Wars*, Macmillan, 2011, p. 351. Clarke was also variously a gun-runner, MP, magistrate, sailor, poet, explorer, revolutionary, secretary and zoologist (Raymond Challinor, *John S. Clarke: Parliamentarian, Poet, Lion-Tamer*, Pluto Press, 1977).

7 www.alicewheeldon.org.

A possible peace?

Lord Lansdowne, memorandum to the Cabinet, 13 November 1916: *The responsibility of those who needlessly prolong such a War is not less than that of those who needlessly provoke it.*[1]

According to Jeremy Paxman, once the war had started 'there was no way of stopping it, any more than you could suddenly make the dead start to walk again'.[2] In fact, a good argument can be made that there were real possibilities for a negotiated peace in the winter of 1917–18.[3]

Indeed, a series of events throughout 1917 and into early 1918 gives credence to the notion that, given a different response on the part of Western political leaders, 'anything m[ight] have been possible'.[4]

These included:
- the revolutions in Russia, the first of which resulted in a call for socialists to discuss peace terms over the heads of their respective governments;
- the July 1917 Reichstag Peace Resolution, adopted by German parliamentarians against the wishes of Germany's High Command;
- the French Army mutinies of May–June 1917;[5]
- the failure of Germany's U-boat offensive to win the war; and
- the massive anti-war strike in Germany between 28 January–3 February 1918.[6]

By the autumn of 1917, several key members of the British cabinet had privately 'made predictions that peace would have to be negotiated sooner or later'.[7]

However, Britain – which had already agreed to expand Allied war aims to include the dissolution of the Turkish and Austro-Hungarian empires, and remained committed to the resolutions of the 1916 Paris Economic Conference, 'to continue economic warfare against the Germans even after they were defeated' – would prove to be a key obstacle to such an outcome.[8]

'Irresistible Pressure'

In a November 1917 memorandum to the Secretary of State, Lord Lansdowne (a former Tory Foreign Secretary and a hawk at the war's outbreak) noted his impression:

'[T]hat the people of Germany and Austria would put irresistible pressure on their governments, and compel them to offer us decent terms, but for the success of those governments in convincing them that decent terms are unobtainable and that England is the sole obstacle in the way.' [9]

Instead, on 4 February 1918, the Allies 'declar[ed] that all prospect of negotiations had now ended and that force would be met with force', derailing 'a concerted effort on the part of [German] moderates… to press for a diplomatic offensive, based on an explicit renunciation of annexation in Belgium, *before* [the German military] was given [its] chance to crash through'. [10]

1   Lloyd George, *War memoirs of Lloyd George*, vol. I, 1938 (?), p. 517.

2   'At the Eleventh Hour', BBC I, first broadcast on 17 February 2014.

3   Douglas Newton, 'The Lansdowne 'Peace Letter' of 1917 and the Prospect of Peace by Negotiation with Germany', *Australian Journal of Politics and History*, vol. 48, no. 1, 2002, pp. 16–39. Among other things, such a peace would have saved the lives and limbs of the scores of thousands killed and wounded during the German offensives of March and April 1918. (David Stevenson, *With Our Backs to the Wall: Victory and Defeat in 1918*, Penguin, 2012, p. 55).

4   Newton, *op. cit.*, p.37.

5   David Stevenson, *1914–1918*, Penguin, 2005, p. 327. Despite having been misled (by Haig and others) about its scale, Lloyd George's War Policy Committee concluded that the crisis in the French army 'was a reflection of a more serious crisis in French political life', and it was the need to 'sustain French national morale' – for fear 'that France might go the same way as Russia' – rather than any faith in Haig's plans, that 'finally persuaded ministers that they had to support an offensive in Flanders' in the mutinies' wake (David French, *The Strategy of the Lloyd George Coalition, 1916–1918*, Oxford University Press, 1995, pp. 117, 121–122). Over 400,000 soldiers were killed or wounded in the resulting carnage (Stevenson, *op. cit.*, p. 336).

6   See p. 86 of this booklet.

7   Newton, *op. cit.*, p. 34.

8   Newton, *op. cit.*, pp. 20–22; Richard Striner, *Woodrow Wilson and World War I*, Rowman & Littlefield, 2014, p. 110.

9   Newton, *op. cit.*, p. 30.

10 *Ibid.*, pp. 33, 37.

The Women's Peace Crusade, 1916–1918

Helen Crawfurd, June 1917:
For nearly three years the war has gone on, and we women have been afraid, afraid to trust our own judgement, afraid to speak, afraid to act... Shall we remain silent any longer?

History has not recorded what Selina Cooper and her daughter Mary thought when, on 11 August 1917, their demonstration demanding 'a people's peace' arrived at Nelson's recreation ground to find a 15,000-strong patriotic mob already there, 'baying for blood and hurling earth and clinkers'.[1]

Their protest was part of the Women's Peace Crusade (WPC), the remarkable grass-roots socialist movement, pressing for peace negotiations to end the war, that 'spread like wildfire across the country' from the summer of 1917 until the Armistice the following year.[2]

'Peace Our Hope'
Earlier that day, roughly 1,200 women and girls had assembled in an open space outside the centre of Nelson, in Lancashire.

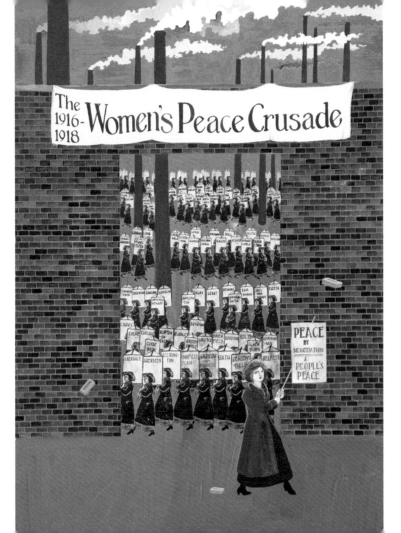

Presumably anticipating trouble, Selina – a long-term feminist and socialist – had placed herself at the front. Behind her stood the members of the Independent Labour Party (ILP) Girls' Guild, with their green banner, 'Peace Our Hope'. In front of her stood a line of mounted police.

Other banners that day read: 'We demand a people's peace'; 'Workers of the world unite for Peace'; and 'Hail the Russian Revolution'. A group of children, their fathers serving in the war, carried one saying simply: 'We want our daddy'.

The crowd lining the route appears to have been largely hostile. Scuffles broke out and, when they finally arrived at the recreation ground, there was a vast throng of counter-demonstrators stretching for as far as the eye could see.

Howled down by the mob – and with only the police presence preventing the speakers from being physically attacked – the rally lasted only forty minutes.

The Women's Peace Crusade

'The first truly popular campaign [in Britain], linking feminism and anti-militarism' [3], the WPC began in Glasgow, where a 1916 protest organised by Helen Crawfurd – a working-class feminist and socialist who had played a significant role in the famous Glasgow Rent Strike of 1915 – drew a crowd of 5,000.

The following year, Crawfurd issued a call for action that was taken up by women across the country: 3,000 attended a meeting in Leeds; 3,000 marched through Bradford; 300 marched in Birmingham (though their banner was torn up); and in Leicester a crowd of 3,000 assembled in the marketplace to listen to an all-woman platform of speakers.

By September 1918 the WPC had 123 branches.[4] In Glasgow it held anti-war meetings at the gates of the shipyards, and Helen Crawfurd and fellow activist Agnes Dollan got 'into the Council Chambers while the Town Council was in session… showering down leaflets on the Councillors, demanding Peace and an end to the carnage.'[5] In Manchester, police banned a WPC leaflet, 'Casualties', so activists travelled to the boundary with Salford (where the leaflet wasn't banned) and leafleted Mancunians crossing the boundary.

'A people's peace'

The Crusade's central demand was 'a people's peace': a negotiated end to the war without annexations or 'crushing indemnities' – real possibilities for which probably existed in the winter of 1917–1918 (see pp. 57–59). However, in the teeth of business-funded mobs and a massive propaganda campaign bankrolled by the Treasury (see pp. 65–68), the odds were always heavily stacked against it.

A fortnight after the Nelson protest, Selina Cooper told a meeting at a local school hall:

'It is one thing to come to a meeting like this; it is another thing to march through the street to be jeered and booed at. We will never forget that demonstration; I think it was something heroic…'

She was right.

1   The account of the Nelson demo is based on the following sources: Jill Liddington, *The Long Road to Greenham* [hereafter 'Long Road'], Virago, 1989, p. 125; Jill Liddington, *The Life and Times of a Respectable Rebel*, pp. 277–280; *Labour Leader*, 16 August 1917.

2   *Long Road*, pp. 117, 109.

3   *Ibid.*, p. 129; 'When making the decision whether or not to go on the 1912 [suffragette] raid, breaking windows down in Whitehall with seven other Scottish suffragettes, [Crawfurd] prayed for a message from her [clergyman] husband's sermon. It turned out to be about Christ making a whip of cords and chasing the money changers out of the temple, and she thought, "If Christ can be Militant so can I!"' (Anne Wiltshire, *Most Dangerous Women*, Pandora, 1985, p. 149).

4   The seventy-seven branches mentioned in the *Labour Leader*, all of whose names are reproduced in the poster, were: Aberdale, Aberdeen, Accrington, Annfield Plain, Barrow-in-Furness, Bath, Beaconsfield, Belfast, Birmingham, Blackburn, Bolton, Bradford, Brierfield, Bristol, Briton-Ferry, Brynmawr, Burnley, Burton-on-Trent, Carlisle, Clydebank, Colne, Corby, Coventry, Cowdenbeath, Cowling, Crosshills – Keighley, Cwmavon, Dalry, Darlington, Derby, Desborough, Douglas Water, Edinburgh, Exeter, Glasgow, Goole, Guildford, Halifax, Heanor, Huddersfield, Hull, Ilkley, Kendal, Kilmarnock, Leeds, Leicester, Liverpool, Lotherdale, London, Long Eaton, Manchester, Market Harborough, Merthyr Tydfil, Nelson, Netherfield, Newcastle, Newport, Northampton, Norwich, Nottingham, Paisley, Port Talbot, Reading, Rotherham, Rothwell, Sheffield, Skelmanthorpe, Shotley Bridge, Southport, Stanley, Sutton-in-Ashfield, Swadlincote, Troedyrhiw, Wakefield, Wellingborough, Wrexham, and Ystradgynlais.

5   Helen Crawfurd, *Unpublished Autobiography*, p. 155.

Stopping the rot

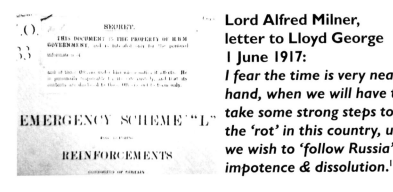

Lord Alfred Milner, letter to Lloyd George 1 June 1917:
I fear the time is very near at hand, when we will have to take some strong steps to stop the 'rot' in this country, unless we wish to 'follow Russia' into impotence & dissolution.[1]

In June 1917 Lord Alfred Milner was a member of Lloyd George's five-man War Cabinet. With his letter he enclosed a memorandum from Victor Fisher, Secretary of the 'patriotic labour' group the British Workers' League (BWL).

'Largely responsible for organising' the BWL – putting Fisher in contact with prominent figures in the government, and arranging funding from the likes of the British Empire Producers Organisation – Milner saw it as a means of directly counter-acting 'mischief makers', by force if necessary, and had made sure that it inherited some of the right-wing pre-war National Service League's professional political organisers, men 'skilled in the arts of rabble-rousing and not afraid of violence'.[2]

Patriot mobs

By 1917 violent patriotic mobs had long been 'one of the central mechanisms by which dissent was contained in wartime Britain'.[3] Indeed, by the end of 1915 Glasgow 'was about the only place in the UK in which this type of violence was not becoming endemic.'[4]

'Not simply the result of spontaneous popular anger', from mid-1915 London saw 'systematic right-wing efforts to... prevent known anti-war leaders from holding political meetings of any kind', with journalists linked to Beaverbrook's *Daily Express* playing a leading role.[5]

Nor were such efforts confined to London. The BWL – which by September 1917 had over 150 branches across the country – was one of the key groups providing organisational form to such mob violence.

Creeping fascism

'Given its reactionary – sometimes nearly hysterical – message, the violent nature of much of its membership, its acceptance of a corporatist social model, and its militaristic, chauvinistic programme, it is not difficult to see the [BWL] as a proto-fascist organisation', notes historian Brock Millman.[6]

It was not the only sign of a creeping fascism. With its 'vertical, corporatist reorganisation of the social, economic and political nation, accomplished through explicit appeals to patriotism as an integrating force beyond class and particular interest' the Lloyd George government was also 'as with so much in the latter years of the First World War... a foretaste of the interwar fascist response'.[7]

The National War Aims Committee

Four days after Milner's letter to Fisher, the War Cabinet decided 'to undertake an active campaign to counteract the pacifist movement', which, it claimed, 'had the field to itself'.[8]

Within months a massive propaganda campaign – the National War Aims Committee (NWAC) – was flooding the country with pro-war propaganda, attempting to convince a war-weary nation of the need to 'do all in its power to assist in carrying on the war to a victorious conclusion'.[9]

Officially an NGO, in reality it was 'almost totally funded by the Treasury', 'receiv[ing] something like £1.2 million' – over £50 million in today's money – 'in subsidy or services from government sources' in the 18 months of its existence.[10]

Emergency Scheme L

By 1918 'many British leaders had come to view revolution as a distinct possibility', and a strong, albeit circumstantial, argument can be made that 175,000 trained surplus troops were kept in Britain during that year, in large part to deal with just such a contingency.[11]

Lists of those to be pre-emptively arrested were drawn up, as was a secret contingency plan – Emergency Scheme L – to deploy 19 infantry brigades into three concentration areas 'located near... regions of chronic unrest'.[12]

Had the war continued much longer who knows what 'strong steps' might have been considered necessary to 'stop the "rot"' and prevent Britain from 'follow[ing] Russia'?[13]

1   Marvin Swartz, *The Union of Democratic Control in British Politics During the First World War*, Oxford University Press, 1971, p. 175.

2   Brock Millman, *Managing Dissent in First World War Britain*, Frank Cass, 2000, pp. 112, 114–115; Adam Hochschild, *To End All Wars*, MacMillan, 2011, p. 178.

3   Millman, *op. cit.*, p. 99.

4   *Ibid.*, p. 56.

5   Jon Lawrence, 'Public space, political space', p. 294 in Jay Winter & Jean-Louis Robert, *Capital Cities at War, vol.2*, Yale University Press, 1992. Alongside Milner, Beaverbrook was a 'silent partner' in the coup that brought Lloyd George to power in December 1916, under whose premiership he would later become Minister of Information (Millman, *op. cit.*, pp. 126–127, 240).

6   *Ibid.*, p. 118.

7   *Ibid.*, p. 176.

8   David Monger, *Patriotism and Propaganda in First World War Britain*, Liverpool University Press, 2014, p. 28.

9   Millman, *op. cit.*, p. 237. By 1918 NWAC propaganda was 'reaching something like six million people weekly' (*ibid.*, p. 240). In October 1917, *Satire* magazine noted that 'The War Aims Committee is going about the country to counteract the insidious propaganda of the pacifists. They are making a great success of it, for nobody knows yet what our war aims are' (File 32, Bundle 3, HO 139/23, Public Record Office).

10 Millman, *op. cit.*, pp. 233–234; http://www.measuringworth.com.

11 Millman, *op. cit.*, Chapter 11, but especially pp. 287, 272.

12 *Ibid.*, pp. 4, 282, 289, 291.

13 '[I]n July and August [1918] hardly anyone in authority expected the fighting to end quickly' (David Stevenson, *1914–1918*, Penguin, 2005, p. 466).

The Tribunal

Lydia Smith:
*When the police went to 'dismantle'
– as they called it – the second
printer, they were jubilant. They
said – they did it very thoroughly,
he wasn't able to start again – and
said 'That will be the end of that'.
And therefore, when we came out
[with] 'Here we are again!!'...
Scotland Yard took it very badly.*[1]

Whenever they had any difficulty in unscrewing a component, they
simply broke it off.[2]

It was 22 April 1918 and the six police officers had been sent to the
printing works of Samuel Street – printer of the No-Conscription
Fellowship (NCF)'s newspaper the *Tribunal* – to break up his
machinery. Before long they had destroyed – or seized – over £500
worth (£25,000 worth in today's money) and were carting off books,
invoices and stationery, in addition to the broken machines.

They never produced a warrant.

'We have done for you this time!'

That same day, the police also swooped on the publishing offices of
the *Tribunal*, a few minutes walk from Trafalgar Square.

When the paper's publisher, Joan Beauchamp, refused to reveal to them the name of the editor, the officers searched the office, seizing a number of books and papers.

'We have done for you this time!', one officer told Lydia Smith, the young head of the NCF's Press Department.[3]

'Here we are again!!'

Nonetheless, three days later the *Tribunal* came out on schedule as a one-page leaflet, cheekily headlined 'Here we are again!!'.

Despite their best efforts, the authorities were never able to shut down the paper, which continued to be printed throughout the remainder of the war. This remarkable achievement was possible because by 1918, with almost all of the NCF's male leadership in jail, the administrative work of the organisation was largely being conducted by a formidable team of women, many of whom had cut their teeth in the pre-war movement for women's suffrage.[4]

In late 1917, the group decided that Beauchamp and Smith would share the work of editing and publishing the paper. Beauchamp would list her name as the publisher – and go to prison if necessary – leaving Smith free to continue the work.[5]

On 22 April, a small handpress, which had been purchased and hidden in the home of a sympathetic printer, was brought into action, and '[f]or almost a year this clandestine press, manned by a volunteer printer and compositor, produced the weekly edition'.[6]

Here we are again!!

CATHERINE MARSHALL
VIOLET TILLARD
JOAN BEAUCHAMP
LYDIA SMITH

Anti-war activists, editors and publishers
of the No-Conscription Fellowship
1915-1920

With Scotland Yard keen to locate the secret press, great care was necessary. 'On at least one occasion the press had to be moved when neighbours began to comment about odd noises', while an impoverished-looking woman with a baby carriage who visited the *Tribunal* office every few days, apparently looking for charity, was actually smuggling proof sheets for the paper in her pram.[7]

Speaking decades later, in an episode of the BBC television programme *Yesterday's Witness*, Smith explained that:

'The [police] took a room opposite us... and kept watch on us... but they never found out, partly because they were so convinced that I was sending in for a man... they couldn't believe that I was the editor...'[1]

About the women named on the poster

Described by the *Labour Leader* as 'the most able woman organiser in the land', Catherine Marshall calculated that she was liable to 2,000 years' imprisonment for her work with the NCF.[8]

Violet Tillard was sentenced to 61 days imprisonment for refusing to divulge the name of the printer of a privately circulated issue of *NCF News*, while Somerset socialist Joan Beauchamp received two prison sentences for her role as the *Tribunal*'s publisher.

Lydia Smith was prosecuted alongside Tillard, though the charges against her were dismissed under the Probation of Offenders Act. Unbeknownst to the authorities she was actually the *Tribunal*'s editor.

All had been active pre-war suffragists.[9]

1 'Prisoners of Conscience: No to the State', *Yesterday's Witness*, first broadcast 26 May 1969, available online at http://www.bbc.co.uk/programmes/p01t27mf

2 Unless otherwise stated, material on the 11 April 1918 raid and subsequent prosecutions is drawn from the following sources: 'Here we again!!', *Tribunal*, 25 April 1918; 'At Bow Street Again', *Tribunal*, 16 May 1918; 'Violet Tillard', *Tribunal*, 15 August 1918; 'Joan Beauchamp – Printer', *Tribunal*, 29 August 1918; 'Our Appeal', *Tribunal*, 17 October 1918; 'Rex v. Beauchamp', *Tribunal*, 8 January 1920.

3 William Chamberlain, *Fighting for Peace: The Story of the War Resistance Movement*, Garland, 1971, p. 70.

4 Brock Millman, *Managing Domestic Dissent in First World War Britain*, Frank Cass, 2000, p. 83.

5 David Boulton, *Objection Overruled*, MacGibbon & Kee, 1967, p. 271.

6 Thomas C. Kennedy, *The Hound of Conscience: A History of the No-Conscription Fellowship, 1914–1918*, p. 249. According to F.L. Carsten, following the April 1918 raid the *Tribunal* 'was henceforth printed in a wooden hut or barn on an estate at Box Hill in Surrey and taken from there to London' (F.L. Carsten, *War Against War: British and German Radical Movements in the First World War*, Batsford, 1982, p. 205).

7 Kennedy, *op. cit.*; Adam Hochschild, *To End All Wars: How the First World War Divided Britain*, MacMillan, 2011, p. 325.

8 Anne Wiltsher, *Most Dangerous Women*, Pandora, 1985, pp. 66, 131.

9 *Ibid.*, p. 4; David Mitchell, *Women on the Warpath*, Jonathan Cape, 1966, p. 339; Laura E. Nym Mayhall, *The Militant Suffrage Movement*, Oxford University Press, 2003, p. 49; Kennedy, *op. cit.*, p. 150. Marshall had been part of the National Union of Women's Suffrage Societies, Tillard was with the Women's Freedom League, and Beauchamp worked with Sylvia Pankhurst in the East End.

Te Puea

Te Puea Herangi:
They tell us to fight for king and country. Well, that's all right. We've got a king. But we haven't got a country. That's been taken off us. Let them give us back our land and then maybe we'll think about it again.[1]

They had been expected.

Indeed, they had been welcomed by a large crowd, including girls playing brass band instruments. But now, in front of the 400 people in the crowded meeting house, the time had come for police Sergeant Waterman and his men to fulfil their mission and arrest the King's brother.

'King George of England has asked the Government of New Zealand to assist in the war with all its men who owe allegiance to the Crown,' he explained, appealing to Princess Te Puea to help him 'identify the men whose names I will read from this list.'[2]

'These people are mine'

Her response had been forthright:

'These people are mine. My voice is their voice. I will not agree to my children going to shed blood… The young men who have been balloted will not go… You can fight your own fight until the end.'

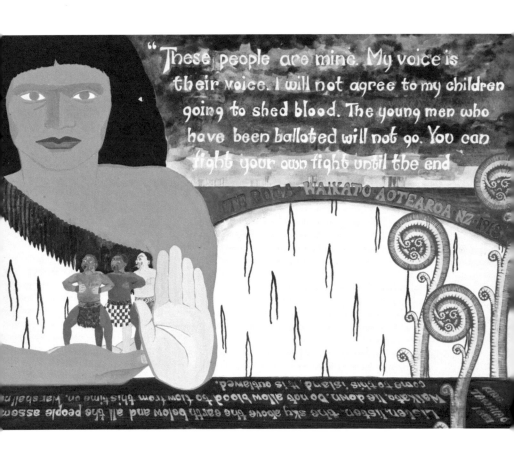

"These people are mine. My voice is their voice. I will not agree to my children going to shed blood. The young men who have been balloted will not go. You can fight your own fight until the end

TE PUEA WAIKATO AOTEAROA NZ 1916

Listen, listen. The sky above, the earth below and all the people assem... Waikato, lie down. Do not allow blood to flow from this time on. War shall ne... come to this island, it is outlawed.

The police then read out the names of the seven men who had failed to show up for medical examination, and, when no-one stepped forward, began to make arrests.

Thus, on 11 June 1918, a new phase began in the Waikato people's remarkable campaign of nonviolent resistance to conscription, led by the Maori princess, Te Puea Herangi.

'The killing of men must stop'

From early on in the war, the Waikato tribes of New Zealand's northern island decided that they would not participate in the Imperial Government's fight, and in 1915 no Waikato volunteers sailed for Europe in either of the first two native contingents.

Te Puea's grandfather, the second Maori King, Tawhiao, had been a pacifist, famously telling the Resident Magistrate in 1881: 'The killing of men must stop'.[3] Thus, in addition to anger over the theft of their land[4], the Waikato also had strong religious and cultural grounds for not volunteering.

When conscription was finally brought in for Maori, in June 1917, it was made plain that it would only apply to the Waikato, who then set about making this as difficult as possible.

Thus, the Inspector of Recruiting Services complained that most young men 'no longer visit towns, but have taken to the country, forests or settlements.' Others foot-dragged, and together these problems 'led to a delay in gathering the first Maori draft, which did not occur until February 1918.'[5]

'I am simply pro-Maori'

After the 11 June 1918 arrests, the police returned repeatedly to arrest more men. Noncooperators were put on a bread and water diet and eventually sentenced to two years' imprisonment with hard labour.

Accused of having German ancestry, Te Puea responded: 'So [does] the British Royal Family. In fact I am neither pro-German nor anti-British. I am simply pro-Maori.'[6]

At war's end no conscripted Maori had served overseas, making the campaign one of the most successful examples of communal resistance to the war, violent or nonviolent.[7]

Indigenous resistance

In all, almost 110,000 indigenous people from the five British 'Dominions' were enlisted into the military during the First World War.[8] Yet, '[t]he social standing of indigenous peoples within the dominant British-based Dominion societies' after the War 'remained one of exclusion and subjugation'.[9]

As the Government exhorts us to celebrate the hundreds of thousands of imperial subjects who, in reality, fought and died 'to defend the very nations and institutions which kept them in subjugation and robbed them of their identities', we should instead be celebrating the stories of those, like the Waikato, who resisted.[10]

1 Michael King, *Te Puea: A Biography*, Hodder and Stoughton, 1977, p. 78.

2 This account of the 11 June 1918 arrests is based on *ibid.*, pp. 88–90, and 'Seven Maori reservists arrested', *Dominion*, 12 June 1918.

3 King, *op. cit.*, p. 77.

4 'The second of the wars of the 1860s [between the New Zealand Government and various Maori tribes] had been contrived by the Government to break the autonomy and grab the land of the Waikato, Maniapoto, and Ngati Haua tribes... The Crown took 887,000 acres of land, mainly Waikato...' (Paul Baker, *King and Country Call*, Auckland University Press, 1988, p. 213).

5 Timothy Wineguard, *Indigenous Peoples of the British Dominions and the First World War*, Cambridge University Press, 2011, p. 159.

6 King, *op. cit.*, p. 95.

7 Wineguard, *op. cit.*, In May 1919 all remaining objectors were released from prison (against military advice), and the 100 unexecuted arrest warrants were annulled.

8 *Ibid.*, p. 264.

9 *Ibid.*, p. 261.

10 Glenford Delroy Howe, *Race, War and Nationalism: A Social History of West Indians in the First World War*, Ian Randle Publishers, 2002, p. xii. The Waikato were certainly not the only indigenous people to resist the war. For example, in Canada in 1917 after conscription was introduced, 'many Indians refused to register', and in some cases 'entire reserves... refused to comply out of defiance, some going so far as to conceal their young men'. (Wineguard, *op. cit.*, pp. 153–154).

Resisting Empire's Call

First World War recruiter in Pretoria, South Africa:
When we speak of joining the overseas contingent our women curse and spit at us, asking us whether the Government, for whom we propose to risk our lives, is not the one which sends the police to our houses at night to pull us and our daughters out of bed and trample upon us.[1]

Desperate to find him, the British had placed his friends and family under surveillance and – after six weeks of unsuccessful hunting – had even offered a substantial reward for his capture.

Like many other Muslims in the north of Nigeria he opposed fighting in the First World War for fear that he might be deployed against his co-religionists in the Ottoman Empire.

A Sergeant in Britain's colonial army, he had persuaded at least twenty other soldiers to join him and then deserted.

But after over four months on the run Tanko Kura was finally captured.[2]

'Who cares about native carriers?'

Britain 'recruited' over a million African 'carriers' during the war. Of these no fewer than 95,000 died from all causes, including malnutrition, disease and overwork – almost twice the number of Australian or Canadian troops who died during the War.[3] One Colonial Office official explained that the East Africa campaign 'only stopped short of a scandal because the people who suffered most were the carriers – and after all, who cares about native carriers?' [4]

As early as 1914, the blood-soaked Governor-General of the Colony and Protectorate of Nigeria, Frederick Lugard, ordered that 'if the emergency is great, carriers must be impressed'.[5] In Nyasaland (today's Malawi), 'There was terror everywhere', Chief Malagengachanzi – a youth at the time – later recalled, 'slavery was the actual way people were taken to war'.[6]

Sometimes 'recruitment' – a euphemism for forced labour – was resisted violently, but such uprisings were swiftly repressed using extreme violence.

Safe havens
But resistance also took other forms.

Throughout Nyasaland, men fled into the bush to avoid being impressed as labourers. 'I escaped and hid in a river and my parents, since I had not married yet, secretly brought food to me,' Vmande Kaombe later recalled.[7]

In some places African elites collaborated with the British. But around Zungeru and along the Cross river in Nigeria, chiefs simply refused to supply any carriers, while the people of Bende Ofufa – a section of the Ikot Ekpene district of south-eastern Nigeria – renounced all alien control, refusing to obey summonses or allow arrests, and the area became a safe haven for those on the run.[8]

Late 20th century Chewa face mask from Malawi. Image © Hans Hillewaert / CC-BY-SA-3.0

Cultural resistance

Once 'recruited', a range of resistance strategies remained, including desertion.

In South Africa, the authorities were forced to take action when it became clear that the number of recruits arriving at the Cape Town mobilisation camp did not tally with the number despatched thither.[9] In the Gold Coast over 10% of soldiers deserted.[10]

In the central region of Nyasaland, the secret religious group known as *nyau* became the focal point for successful resistance to forced military labour.

Members would hide in caves or graveyards connected with the group's rituals – or hide in their own small hole in the bush and don animal masks connected with nyau – knowing that many recruiters were nyau members and that the group's vows required members to aid one another.[11]

Resisting Empire's call

Sergeant Tanko Kura was finally captured, but the following month he escaped again – this time, it seems, permanently.

Launching the government's flagship programme celebrating 'the crucial contribution of the Commonwealth countries during the First World War', David Cameron declared that: 'They fought... defend[ing] the freedoms we enjoy today.' [12]

This dishonest framing of the grotesque realities of imperial history should be a spur to all of us to recover the stories of those, like Sergeant Kura, who resisted Empire's call.

1   Albert Grundlingh, *Fighting Their Own War*, Raven Press, 1987. p. 70.

2   James K. Matthews, 'Reluctant Allies: Nigerian Responses to Military Recruitment 1914–1918', pp. 107–108 in Melvin E. Page (ed), *Africa and the First World War*, MacMillan Press, 1987.

3   Edward Paice, *Tip and Run*, Orion, 2006, p. 392. Even the carrier deaths were only the tip of the iceberg. Scorched-earth tactics and the massive manpower drain caused by 'recruitment' (by Germany as well as Britain) led to a 'severe impairment of the capacity for survival of those left behind', causing hundreds of thousands more deaths (Bill Nasson, 'British Imperial Africa', pp. 146–147, in Robert Gerwarth & Erez Manela (eds), *Empires at War: 1911–1923*, Oxford University Press, 2014; Paice, *op. cit.*, pp. 392, 394, 398).

4   *Ibid.*, p.393.

5   Matthews, *op. cit.*, p. 98. In 1906 Lugard had sent a 500-man column to 'annihilate' the Nigerian village of Satiru, killing 2,000 people (Thomas Pakenham, *The Scramble for Africa*, Abacus, 2001, pp. 651–652).

6   Melvin Page, *The Chiwaya War* [hereafter 'Chiwaya'], Westview, 2000, p. 49.

7   *Ibid.*, p. 50.

8   Matthews, *op. cit.*, pp. 98, 104.

9   Grundlingh, op. cit., p. 69.

10 David Killingray, 'Military and Labour Politics in the Gold Coast', p. 162 in Melvin E. Page (ed), *Africa and the First World War*, MacMillan Press, 1987.

11 *Chiwaya*, pp. 50–52.

12 'Commonwealth contribution to First World War to be commemorated', Department for Communities and Local Government press release, 8 November 2013.

Gandhi goes recruiting [1]

Given his reputation, one might imagine that Gandhi would have led a strong campaign of resistance to the war. In reality, he attempted to recruit 12,000 Indians for the war, telling them that if they were not prepared to make this sacrifice 'for the sake of [independence]… we should be regarded unworthy of it'. Fortunately, he was spectacularly unsuccessful: after one month he had fewer than 100 volunteers.

1 Kathryn Tidrick, *Gandhi: A Political and Spiritual Life*, I.B. Tauris, 2006, pp. 128–132.

2 Fenner Brockway, *Bermondsey Story,* Allen & Unwin, 1949, pp. 67–68; 'Why he will not fight: A Negro's argument', *Tribunal*, 19 October 1916.

'My country is divided' [2]

Six feet 6½ inches tall, a skilled carpenter, and the grandchild of a slave on a Jamaican sugar plantation, Isaac Hall arrived in Britain shortly before the war began.

Sentenced to two years hard labour for refusing to fight, he explained his resistance as follows:

'My country is divided up among the European Powers (now fighting against each other) who in turn have oppressed and tyrannised over my fellow-men… In view of these circumstances, and also the fact that I have a moral objection to all wars, I would sacrifice my rights rather than fight…'

Richard Müller and the Revolutionary Shop Stewards

Richard Müller, 16 December 1918:
All political questions are in the end questions of power.[1]

There were already police informers at the dance-hall so the small group decamped to a pub in Sophienstrasse.

There, a man with a toothbrush moustache proposed a strike for the following day, when Karl Liebknecht – Germany's most famous anti-war campaigner – would be on trial for treason for denouncing the war and the government at a May Day demonstration.

This was agreed and the next day, 28 June 1916, some 55,000 munitions workers marched in perfect discipline through the streets of Berlin shouting 'Long live Liebknecht!' and 'Long live peace!'.[2]

Over the next 2½ years the man with the moustache would organise two more anti-war strikes and play a leading role in the overthrow of the centuries-old Hohenzollern dynasty. His name was Richard Müller, leader of a clandestine network within the German Metalworkers Union (DMV) that would later call itself the Revolutionary Shop Stewards.

Collaboration and resistance

The biggest party in the German Parliament, the socialist Social Democratic Party of Germany (SPD) had traditionally 'proclaimed [its] opposition to war from the rooftops'.[3] However, as soon as the war began, the SPD rapidly ditched its socialist internationalism and backed the war effort. The major unions did likewise.

Not everyone followed suit.

In December 1914, Karl Liebknecht became the first SPD delegate to vote against war credits, and opposition was also secretly organised inside the DMV, the largest trade union in the world, starting in Berlin. There, unbeknownst to the union's leadership, 'the lathe operators organised allegedly apolitical pub evenings or met privately after the official union sessions', gradually building a covert oppositional network within the union.[4]

'Class cancelled because of revolution'[5]

The June 1916 strike was a turning point. The first political mass strike of the war to take place in Germany, it would be followed by two more, in April 1917 and January 1918, involving 300,000 and 500,000 people respectively.

An estimated 50,000 strikers were sent to the front in the wake of the January 1918 strike, and the Stewards began stockpiling weapons for an armed revolt. But it was the sailors, not the workers, who would begin the German Revolution.

Revolutionary
Shop
Stewards

GERMANY 1916-1919

Müller
Richard

'[A] consequence, not a cause, of Germany's defeat'[6], the revolution began with a naval mutiny at Wilhelmshaven, which in turn led to a series of virtually bloodless uprisings throughout Germany.

Finally, on 9 November 1918, the revolution came to Berlin.

Here the Stewards' systematic preparation was critical. Müller feared that the army would 'drown the people's revolution in blood', but the workers carried placards saying 'Brothers, no shooting!', and 'hardly a soldier was prepared to fire on them'.[7]

A revolution betrayed

The overthrow of the monarchy ushered in a new struggle, pitting revolutionaries like Müller against the SPD's leadership, who now chose to collaborate with 'the most reactionary sections of German society, the officer corps and the state bureaucracy', in order to prevent revolutionary change.[8]

On 9 November, the SPD's chairman, Friedrich Ebert, was made Chancellor. That evening he was informed that the officer corps expected the new government to 'fight against Bolshevism' and that it placed itself at his disposal 'for such a purpose'.[9] Ebert would have no problem with this.

The revolutionaries' hopes were ultimately crushed using massive violence, though the fetishisation of armed struggle on the part of some of them probably also contributed to their failure.[10]

'Germany became a democracy – but a democracy in which the bastions of power were held by the adherents of the old regime… [until] finally they succeeded in destroying it by handing over political power to [Hitler]'.[11]

1   Ralf Hoffrogge, *Working-Class Politics in the German Revolution*, Brill, 2014 [hereafter, 'Hoffrogge 1'], p. 90.

2   F.L. Carsten, *War Against War*, Batsford, 1982, p. 83.

3   *Ibid.*, p. 13.

4   Ralf Hoffrogge, 'From Unionism to Workers' Councils' [hereafter, 'Hoffrogge 2'], p. 87 in Immanuel Ness & Dario Azzellini (eds), *Ours to Master and to Own: Workers' Control from the Commune to the Present*, Haymarket, 2011. p. 91.

5   Note in Einstein's lecture diary for 9 November 1918 (Walter Isaacson, *Einstein: His Life and Universe*, Pocket Books, 2007, p. 240).

6   David Stevenson, *1914–1918*, Penguin, 2005, p. 499.

7   Murray Bookchin, *The Third Revolution, vol. 4*, Continuum International, 2005, p.23; Hoffrogge 1, pp. 68–69.

8   Harry Harmer, *Rosa Luxemburg*, Haus, 2008, p. 124.

9   *Ibid.*

10 The 'Spartacist Uprising' of January 1919 – again primarily the work of the Stewards – is a case in point. Beginning as a general strike involving hundreds of thousands of workers, it rapidly evolved into a 'revolutionary uprising' involving less than 1,000 armed fighters (*Hoffrogge 1*, pp. 100–106; email from Ralf Hoffrogge, 21 March 2014). Significantly, Hoffrogge notes that 'Although the majority of workers supported the general strike… only a minority supported the armed uprising; after the devastation of World War 1, violence in political struggles was unpopular, even among the most radical workers' (*Hoffrogge 2*, p. 97 n.15). Müller had opposed the move as being premature (*Hoffrogge 1*, p. 102).

11 Carsten, *op. cit.*, p. 232.

Lift the Hunger Blockade!

Catherine Marshall, May 1919: *Only in freedom is permanent peace possible.*[1]

It must have been a strange sight: the ex-suffragette leading a procession of soldiers four-abreast down Whitehall, under a banner reading 'Lift the Hunger Blockade!'

The Women's International League (WIL)[2] had announced a demonstration in Trafalgar Square, against the continuing blockade of Germany and Austria-Hungary, to take place on 6 April 1919. One of the most bellicose daily papers had launched an advance attack on the event, 'call[ing] upon soldiers to come and break it up'.[3]

They turned up in force, but the paper had failed to reckon with the persuasive powers of the speakers, including the veteran feminist and anti-war campaigner Emmeline Pethick-Lawrence.

A resolution to end the blockade was passed with enthusiasm by the ten-thousand-strong crowd, who then demanded to know what would be done with it. 'I will take it to Downing Street if the army will come with me,' Pethick-Lawrence replied, and they agreed to join her.

'Until the Germans learn a few things'

In place since 1914, Britain's illegal naval blockade of Germany 'sought to starve the whole population – men, women, and children, old and young, wounded and sound – into submission' (Churchill), and may have been responsible for as many as three quarters of a million deaths during the war.[4]

After the armistice was signed on 11 November 1918, '[t]he blockade was maintained strictly until March [1919] and more leniently until July, leading to perhaps a quarter of a million civilian deaths.'[5] 'British officials took the view that they didn't want to relax the blockade "until the Germans learn a few things".'[6]

Others saw matters differently – and not just about the hunger blockade. Indeed, many of those who had struggled to end the war now turned their attention to other causes, including disarmament[7], opposing Western military intervention against the Soviet Union, and the struggle against fascism.

A preventable catastrophe?

Though it may be true that 'the Second World War would have been inconceivable without the First, the earlier war did not lead inevitably to the later one'.[8]

Indeed, Noam Chomsky has even speculated that the Second World War could have been prevented as late as 1938, but wasn't 'mainly because Britain and the United States weren't that much opposed to [Hitler].'[9]

1 Anne Wiltsher, *Most Dangerous Women*, Pandora, 1985, p. 210.

2 The League was the British section of the International Committee of Women for Permanent Peace (ICWPP), established at the 1915 Women's International Congress at the Hague (Wiltsher, *op. cit.*, pp. 126, 131).

3 Emmeline Pethick-Lawrence, *My Part in a Changing World*, Gollancz, 1938, p. 325.

4 Nicholson Baker, *Human Smoke*, Simon and Schuster, 2008, p.2; C. Paul Vincent, *The Politics of Hunger*, Ohio University Press, 1985, p. 141.

5 David Stevenson, *1914–1918*, Penguin, 2005, p. 512.

6 Stephen Shalom, *Imperial Alibis*, South End Press, 1993, p. 119.

7 At the ill-fated 1932 World Disarmament Conference, Germany proposed a total prohibition on bombing, but Britain insisted on exempting bombing for 'police purposes in certain outlying regions' (Sven Linqvist, *A History of Bombing*, Granta, 2001, section 140). '[W]e insisted on reserving the right… to bomb niggers!', Lloyd George later observed (Frances Stevenson, *Lloyd George: A Diary*, Hutchinson & Co, 1971, p. 259).

8 Stevenson, *op. cit.*, p. 503.

9 'On War and Activism: Noam Chomsky interviewed by Charngchi Way', 9 December 2005, http://www.chomsky.info/interviews/20051209.htm. According to Chomsky, 'The rise of fascism in the interwar period… was generally regarded rather favourably by the US and British governments' as 'the fascist version of extreme nationalism permitted extensive Western economic penetration and also destroyed the much-feared labor movements and the left' (Noam Chomsky, *Hegemony or Survival*, Metropolitan Books, 2003, p. 67).

Epilogue

Cornel West: *It takes tremendous courage to think for yourself... William Butler Yeats used to say it takes more courage to examine the dark corners of your own soul than it does for a soldier to fight on the battlefield. Courage to think critically... Courage to think, courage to love, courage to hope.*[1]

One of the most disturbing things about the First World War is that, at least at the outset, it appears to have been carried out in 'a sense of defiant duty, rather than a jingoistic desire for war'.[2]

Thus one recent academic study concludes that in 1914, 'ordinary British and Irish people... did not back the war because they were deluded, brainwashed, and naively duped into an idiotic bloodbath', but rather that 'their support was very often carefully considered, well-informed, reasoned, and only made once all other options were exhausted.'[3]

A kind of civic faith

Viewed from a more radical perspective, this suggests that much of the vital spade work needed to create public support had already taken place long before July 1914.

During the quarter century leading up to the war, the British labour movement's peace campaign sought 'to defy a group of profoundly powerful ideas about patriotism and Empire, a set of beliefs which had gained such wide acceptance across the boundaries of class and religion that they could be deemed the fundamentals of a kind of civic faith.' [4] With their meagre resources, peace campaigners were pitted against opponents 'with abundant resources and technologies on hand, who ceaselessly propagated ultra-patriotic, imperialist, and militarist values.' [5]

Breaking free

It is hard not to recognise some telling similarities with our current situation, suggesting some important lessons for contemporary peace campaigners. [6]

Now as then, what Noam Chomksy has termed 'the bounds of thinkable thought' within the dominant intellectual culture are extremely narrow, and ideas such as Britain being 'a force for good in the world' that 'should intervene abroad when other people's rights and freedom are threatened' play a crucial role in mobilising public support – or at least acquiescence – for military action. [7]

The First World War's opponents were often able to break free of ruling propaganda assumptions by appealing to transnational (or, in the case of resisters in the Global South, anti-imperial) forms of solidarity rooted in class, race, gender, religious belief or abstract ideals such as 'civilisation'.

During these centenary years, their struggles remain one of the few things worth celebrating.

1 Astra Taylor (dir), *The Examined Life* (2008).

2 Catriona Pennell, *A Kingdom United*, Oxford University Press, 2014, p. 5, referring to the attitudes of the French and German populations in 1914.

3 Pennell, *op. cit.*, p. 4. In reality, all other options were *never* exhausted (see pp. 21–23 and 57–59 of this booklet).

4 Douglas Newton, *British Labour, European Socialism and the Struggle for Peace, 1889–1914*, Oxford University Press, 1985, p. 340.

5 *Ibid.*

6 Bertrand Russell's reflections on his time in the WWI peace movement ('Some Psychological Difficulties of Pacifism in Wartime', 1935) will also resonate with contemporary activists eg. his reference to 'some men' in whom 'the habit of standing out against the herd became so ingrained that they could not co-operate with anybody about anything' or his experiences of attending meetings 'nominally opposed to all war [where] the threat of violent revolution was applauded to the echo.'

7 Noam Chomsky, *Necessary Illusions*, Pluto Press, 1989, pp. 10 -11, 59. In an October 2014 poll, 72% of Britons agreed that 'Britain is a force for good in the world', while 47% agreed that Britain 'should intervene abroad when other people's rights and freedom are threatened' ('Six in ten back UK military intervention against IS', Ipsos-MORI, 23 October 2014). For a survey of the grim realities of Britain's post-WW2 foreign policy, drawing on declassified government files, see Mark Curtis, *Web of Deceit*, Vintage, 2003.

Acknowledgements

We would like to thank the Joseph Rowntree Charitable Trust, the Lipman-Miliband Trust and the Amiel and Melburn Trust for their financial support for this project, and Quaker Peace and Social Witness for donating the room for our launch event.

We would also like to thank the following people for their help, ideas and inspiration: Maciej J. Bartkowski, Jennifer Bell, Bill Hetherington, Adam Hochschild, Ralf Hoffrogge, Susan Johns, Zaven Khatchaturian, Mark Kosman, Gabrielle Lewry, Chloe Mason, Andrea Needham, Douglas Newton, Ann Parsonson, Silu Pascoe, Milan Rai, Alison Ronan, Erica Smith and Emma Sangster.

Thanks also to the librarians and archivists at the Alexander Turnbull Library, British Library, Imperial War Museum, LSE, King's College Library, McMaster University, Museum of London, National Library of Ireland, Public Record Office, Senate House Library, and UCL SSEES.

Little or nothing in this booklet is original to us. The work of the following authors has been of especial importance: Ralf Hoffrogge, Michael King, Leah Levenson, Jill Liddington, Brock Millman, Douglas Newton, Sheila Rowbotham, Jo Vellacott, and Anne Wiltsher.

Emily would also like to thank Annie Rae for giving her Winifred McKenzie's wood engraving tools, which were used to make the wood engraving parts of the posters.

Last but not least we would like to thank our generous Kickstarter backers:
Paul Allard, Mark Ashmore, Badger Housing Co-op, Veronica Ball, Jennifer Bell, Martin Birdseye, Chris Booth, Andii Bowher, Luci Carolan, Lucy Craig, Nigel Danby, Andrea D'Cruz, Miriam Dobson, Rona Drennan, George Alan Gerrard, John Gittings, Sid Gould, Lesley Grahame, Brian Guthrie, Maggie Holdsworth, Rachel Holtom, Tony Holroyde, Simon Hughes, Salih Ibrahim, Fiona Joseph, Sarah Lasenby, Rachel Lever, John Lynes, Doro Marden, Anabel Marsh, John Morris, Andrea Needham, Guy Nicholls, Patrick Nicholson, Abby Nicol, Luke Parks, David Polden, Maciej Poplawski, Colin Prescod, Ann Ray, Karen Redfern, Nick Rendle, Sally Reynolds, Anna Robinson, Diana Shelley, Robbie Spence, Jonathan Stevenson, Robert Stuart, Isobel Urquhart, Bridget Walker, Marie Walsh, David Charles Webb, Anthony Webster, Martina Weitsch, Paul Wesley, and Joan E West.

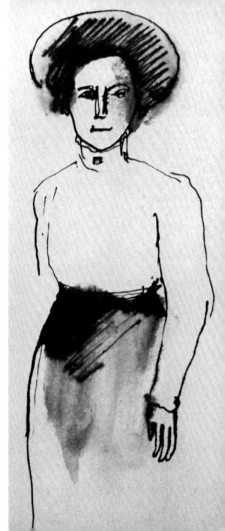